101 Am
Do in Croatia

Introduction

So you're going to Croatia, huh? You are very very lucky indeed! You are sure in for a treat because Croatia is, without a doubt, one of the most special travel destinations in Europe – the world even! It offers something for every visitor, so whether you are into exploring the local gastronomic scene, ogling at ancient fortresses and palaces, or immersing yourself in the incomparable Croatian coastline, this country has something that you'll treasure.

This guide will take you on a journey to all the hotspots of Croatia such as Dubrovnik, Split, Hvar, Zagreb, Vis Island, Pag Island, Pula, and loads more places besides.

In this guide, we'll be giving you the low down on:
- the very best things to shove in your pie hole, whether you want to chow down on a traditional Croatian octopus salad, or you'd like to sip on Croatian wines
- incredible festivals, from electronic festivals with world famous headliners through to the Pula Film Festival, which is hosted in a Roman amphitheatre dating to the 1st century

- the coolest historical and cultural sights that you simply cannot afford to miss like the city walls of Dubrovnik and prehistoric caves with imposing stalactites
- the most incredible outdoor adventures, whether you want to ride the rapids of the Cetina River, or you fancy having windsurfing lessons in the coastal town of Bol
- where to shop for authentic souvenirs so that you can remember your trip to Croatia forever
- the places where you can party like a local and make new friends
- and tonnes more coolness besides!

Let's not waste any more time – here are the 101 most amazing, spectacular, and coolest things not to miss in Croatia!

1. Have a Wine Tasting Experience on Hvar Island

If you are a wine lover, you might wonder if Croatia has any wine culture at all. While it's true that Croatian wines do not have much in the way of worldwide acclaim, there's actually a very vibrant wine producing culture that you should definitely make the effort to explore. One of our favourite wineries is on the island of Hvar, and is called Plenkovic Winery. It's situated on steep south facing slopes, so you'll have a stellar view of the ocean while you sip on Croatian wine.

(www.zlatanotok.hr)

2. Stroll Dubrovnik's City Walls

Probably the most famous sight of Dubrovnik is its city walls. These defensive stone walls extend for 2 kilometres, and have protected Dubrovnik since way back in the 7th century but have been added to in the many centuries since then. These stone walls are some of the largest, most comprehensive, and best preserved in all of Europe. It's possible to walk the entire length of the city walls and get a truly immersive sense of the city's history while you do so.

(http://citywallsdubrovnik.hr/bastina/gradske-zidine/?lang=en)

3. Gorge on Hvar's Signature Dish, Gregada

Before you head to Croatia, you might not be entirely sure about what Croatian food actually is. And the truth is that it has many different influences, and can be really quite different as you travel to different parts of the country. But on the islands, it's always fish and seafood for the win. On the beautiful island of Hvar, we enjoy an island dish called gregada, which is basically a fish stew. It can be made with whatever is caught that day, and is flavoured with parsley, olive oil, onions, potatoes, and garlic.

4. Stroll the Colourful Aisles of Dolac Market

For us, one of the best way to explore the local culture of a new town or city is to stroll the aisles of one of the local markets, and there's certainly no shortage of charming markets to explore across Croatia. In Zagreb, we are particularly fond of Dolac Market, a farmer's market with a wealth of colourful produce, and only a moment's stroll from the main square. As well as vibrant fruits and veggies, we adore the homemade corn bread you can find.

(Dolac 9, 10000, Zagreb; www.trznice-zg.hr/default.aspx?id=298)

5. Eat Traditional Dalmation Food in an Abandoned Village

If you're a foodie, Croatia might not be the first country in Europe that you would think of visiting, but we think that it's an incredibly underrated food destination. One of our favourite spots to eat authentic Dalmation food is Konoba Humac, a restaurant that you'll find in an abandoned village – it's pretty much the only thing there. The house specialties are lamb, veal, and octopus, and we think that their barbecue style of cooking makes everything taste extra delicious.

(www.facebook.com/Konoba-Humac-357534557644483)

6. Escape the Tourist Traps and Relax on Sveti Jakov Beach

Croatia is a destination that attracts many people who want to avoid the more crowded beaches that you'll find in European countries like Italy and Spain, but it's possible to get off the beaten track of the beaten track itself by choosing particularly isolated beaches within Croatia. If you would prefer not to jostle for towel space, and you'd like to enjoy perfect peace and tranquillity, be sure to check out Sveti Jakov beach. It's reachable from Dubrovnik but not on the tourist radar whatsoever. *(Ul. Vlaha Bukovca 14, 20000)*

7. Feel All Lovey Dovey at Casanova Fest

Love is what makes the world go round, right? Well, as if the landscapes and cityscapes of Croatia were not filled with enough romance, there is a whole festival in Croatia that is dedicated to the magic of love: Casanova Fest. The festival is located in Vrsar-Orsera, because this was a place that Casanova was said to have visited twice. Love and romance is explored through readings, talks, films, performances, gastronomic events, and more during the festival, which takes place every June.

(www.casanovafestvrsar.com)

8. Pay a Visit to the Roman Amphitheatre in Pula

For Ancient Roman sights, you might think that you need to travel to Italy. But you should remember that Croatia is only a short boat ride away from Italy, and this means that you can discover some gems of ancient history there too. Take the 1st century Roman amphitheatre of the city of Pula, for example. This magnificent structure is made entirely from limestone, and was used to host Gladiatorial contests with up to 20,000 spectators at any one time. *(Scalierova ul. 30, 52100, Pula; www.ami-pula.hr/hr/dislocirane-zbirke/amfiteatar/amfiteatar)*

9. Drink Your Cares Away With a Glass of Rakija

Poland has its vodka, Spain has sherry, and Mexico has tequila, but what about Croatia? Is there any particular drink in this country that stands apart from the crowd and that's something you should definitely try as a matter of national interest? Indeed there is, and it's called Rakija. This is a fruit brandy that is little known outside of south Europe but is very popular in Croatia. The most common fruits used to flavour the brandy are plums and apricots.

10. Sail Around the Unspoiled Pakleni Islands

Many people choose to visit the islands of Croatia in order to party the night away in a beautiful setting, and who can blame them? But if you are after beauty without the all night parties, you might want to discover some of the lesser explored nooks and crannies of Croatia such as the Pakleni Islands. You can take a boat to these islands from Hvar town, and they offer perfectly unspoiled beaches and bays for peaceful strolling and swimming.

11. Take in the Aromas of Hvar's Annual Lavender Festival

Something that you might not know about Croatia is that it's one of the most aromatic countries on the face of the planet, growing all kinds of deliciously scented herbs and flowers. For a heady experience for the nose, you can't beat the annual Lavender Festival on the island of Hvar. You'll be blown away by the number of things that can be scented and flavoured with lavender, and we are particularly fond of the lavender ice cream. The festival takes place every June.

12. Feel the Heartbreak of the Museum of Broken Relationships

In our opinion, Zagreb is a really great city for museum hopping, and the most unique museum of them all in the Croatian capital would have to be the Museum of Broken Relationships. This might not be the place to be if you're going through some personal heartbreak, but otherwise it's quirky and fascinating. We love the "confessional" part of the museum, where you can leave your own objects and messages related to your own personal heartbreak.

(Ćirilometodska ul. 2, 10000, Zagreb; https://brokenships.com)

13. Enjoy a Taste of Traditional Croatia and Try Peka

When you're on the Dalmatian coast, something that you have to try at least once is a piping hot bowlful of Peka. This is more winter than summer food, but it's the main dish of Dalmatia so we implore you try it no matter what time of year you happen to be in Croatia. What makes this dish different is that it's cooked on hot coals and covered with an iron lid. It comprises a mix of veal or lamb with veggies and Mediterranean flavours courtesy of olive oil, bay leaves, and rosemary.

14. Be Transported to the Croatian Renaissance at Tvrdalj Castle

While you're on Hvar Island, be sure to drag yourself away from the beach for a day, and explore the magnificent Tvrdalj Castle, which you'll find in the small town of Stari Grad. This 16th century fortress was the summer residence of an acclaimed Croatian poet called Petar Hektorovic, and it's very well preserved after all these centuries. The interior courtyard contains a seawater fish pool, and behind the fortress walls, you'll find a herb garden.

(Priko b.b., 21460, Stari Grad)

15. Feel Your Mortality at Mirogoj Cemetery

Okay, we know that you aren't travelling all the way to Croatia to stroll around graveyards, but truthfully, the Mirogoj Cemetery in Zagreb is one of the most spectacular cemeteries that we have ever seen, and we really think that it's worth an hour or two of your time. Something very lovely about the cemetery is that all religious groups are welcome to be buried there, and it is the resting place of many famous Croatians such as Hugo Ehrlich, an architect, and Petar Preradovic, a military general and poet.

(Aleja Hermanna Bollea 27, 10000, Zagreb;
www.gradskagroblja.hr)

16. Be Wowed by the Glowing Blue Cave of Bisevo

Something that we love so much about Croatia is the number of natural attractions it has, and that most of the world know nothing about. If you really want an adventure you won't forget in a hurry, take a tour to the Blue Cave, located within a bay on the island of Bisevo. The reason why it's so special is that blue light is emitted from the cave during certain times of day. For maximum illumination, the best time to be there is around 11am. *(www.tz-komiza.hr)*

17. Party in the Streets During Cest is D'Best Festival

Zagreb is a city with bags of charm at any time of year, but we think that it's particularly vibrant during early June when the Cest is D'Best Festival takes place. This is a street performance festival that transforms the whole city into one giant stage. You'll be able to find everything from circus performances through to live jazz concerts in the middle of the streets and in the city parks.

18. Discover the Underwater World of the Taranto Wreck

If you are something of a water baby, there is plenty of coastline to explore in Croatia, but how much cooler would it be if you could actually make your way underneath the waters? When you think of diving you probably think of tropical climes and colourful sea life, but the coast of Dubrovnik offers a point of difference. Dive off the coast of Dubrovnik and you'll be able to check out the Taranto Wreck – a merchant vessel that was built in 1899 and sank in the 1940s. The wreck is now home to many underwater species, including octopus, lobster, and scorpion fish.

19. Step Back in Time at Trakoscan Castle

If you can tear yourself away from the islands and make it to northern Croatia, you'll discover a fairy tale castle perched in the hilltops called Trakoscan Castle. This castle dates all the way back to the 13th century, created as a defensive fortification, but the original owner of the castle is still unknown, although it now belongs to the Croatian government. Be sure to check out this beautiful structure and the lake in front, which you are sure to enjoy whether you are a history buff or not.

(Trakošćan 1, 42253, Trakošćan; www.trakoscan.hr)

20. Enjoy the 22 Sandy Beaches of Lopar Village

If you are the kind of person who just can't get enough of beach life, golden sands, and clear waters, then Croatia is the most definitely the country for you. Of course, there are beaches in places like Dubrovnik and Split, but if you want to find your own private hideaway, we recommend that you find your way to the village of Lopar on Rab island. There's an astonishing 22 beaches in just one village, many of which are sandy, and you definitely won't be fighting other tourists for towel space.

21. Feel Artsy at the Croatian Museum of Naïve Art

The basic idea of naïve art is that it's artwork created by somebody without the formal training of an art school or a mentor, and indeed there are many famous naïve artists you will have heard of such as Henri Rousseau. In Zagreb, you can find a whole museum dedicated to naïve artists, and most of the 1900 artworks on display have been created by local Croatian artists too. As you walk through the museum aisles, you'll discover works of Surrealism, Cubism, Expressionism, and more, and everything is so much more impressive when you consider that each of the artworks was borne of a desire to create without any formal training whatsoever.

(Ćirilometodska ul. 3, 10000, Zagreb; www.hmnu.hr)

22. Try Croatia's Typical Black Risotto, Crni Rizot

One of the things that surprises many of the people who travel to Croatia for the first time is just how incredible the food is, and how much variety is on offer. It is perfectly sandwiched between East and West Europe, and with some great coastline so the food is actually very impressive indeed. By the coast, something you should definitely order is Crni Rizot. This is a type of local risotto, and the difference with this dish is that the risotto is black and coloured with squid ink, and flavoured with lots of squid itself.

23. Climb to the Bell Tower of Split's Cathedral

We are going to be bold and say that Split Cathedral is one of the most original and spectacular cathedrals that we have seen in Europe. For a start, this cathedral dates way back to the Roman times and was later claimed by Christians in the 5th century. And its octagonal shape makes it unlike any other cathedral that we have seen before. Split is a very beautiful city, so be sure to buy a ticket to climb the belfry tower from where you'll have an incredible view over the city and ocean beyond.

(Ul. Kraj Svetog Duje 5, 21000, Split)

24. Shop for Goodies at Istrian Lifestyle Handmade & Gourmet Fair

If you want to get off the beaten track while you're in Croatia, the lesser explored Istria region is full of surprises. We particularly like Rabac with its small fishing town feel, and the Istrian Lifestyle Handmade & Gourmet Fair that it plays host to each and every summer. Some highlights from the fair include the olive oil, which is made in the region and is said to be some of the best in the world, fresh and dried figs, and even some local wines from family wineries. It's a perfect spot for some gift shopping.

(www.croatia.hr/en-GB/Activities-and-attractions/Events/NewEvents/Istrian-Lifestyle-Handmade-and-Gourmet-Fair-0)

25. Go Ziplining Over the Cetina River

There are people who enjoy ambling around museums, and people who enjoy immersing themselves in nature with thrilling activities. If you are the latter kind of person, one of the heart pumping thrills that you can enjoy while in Croatia is a ziplining adventure over the picturesque Cetina River. You'll be 150 metres above the river, and you'll reach speeds of 65 kilometres per hour so this is not for the faint hearted.

26. Get to Grips With Zagreb at the Zagreb City Museum

Zagreb is one of those cities where you can get a sense of its local history just by walking the cobbled streets and ogling the impressive buildings. But if you would like to be a little bit more informed about all the historic beauty of the city, the Zagreb City Museum is the place to get a comprehensive education. The museum has an astounding

75,000 objects that pertain to the cultural, artistic, political, and economic history of Zagreb. Think paintings, flags, furniture, military uniforms, maps, and loads more besides. *(Opatička ul. 20, 10000, Zagreb; www.mgz.hr)*

27. Explore 200km of Walking Trails in Paklenica National Park

If you are the kind of person who gets bored by sitting on the beach and drinking cocktails, there are plenty of opportunities to get active while you're in Croatia and really immerse yourself in the incredible landscapes of the country. And it doesn't get more beautiful than Paklenica National Park, where you will find 200 kilometres of stunning hiking trails. There are two dolomite limestone canyons to explore, and the Velebit mountain range, which is the largest mountain range in all of Croatia. *(www.np-paklenica.hr)*

28. Indulge a Foodie at Losinj Culinary Festival

Let's face it – one of the highlights of travelling to a new place is filling your stomach with incredible food and drink. If you are restaurant hopping every day, this can get pretty expensive. But if you visit the Losinj Culinary Festival, you'll have the chance to try lots of food, and all in one place so you can save your pennies for some other holiday activities. There are many events throughout the festival such as food walking tours and local wine presentations.

29. Stay in a Treehouse in Cadmos Village

Are you the kind of person who feels most alive when you are in the midst of all of nature's glory? If so, the confines of a whitewashed hotel room isn't going to be an environment that does it for you, and we'd love to recommend some alternative treehouse accommodation in the small village of Cadmos. Although they are in nature, each treehouse is also very well furnished and equipped, and with terraces that overlook the stunning Konavle Valley.

(www.cadmosvillage.com)

30. Indulge a History Buff at the Museum of Croatian Archaeological Monuments

History buffs will have the time of their lives in Croatia, from the castles to cathedrals, and even prehistoric caves. And one place to get an education about the lives of Croats in the Middle Ages is the Museum of Croatian Archaeological Monuments in Split, which is dedicated to showcasing artefacts and remains from the 7th to the 15th centuries. Inside you can explore a 3000 piece collection with items such as weapons, tools, and sculptures.

(Šetalište Ivana Meštrovića 18, 21000, Split; www.mhas-split.hr)

31. Tuck Into Lashings of Brudet, Croatian Fish Stew

With so much glorious coastline, seafood lovers will be in Seventh Heaven on their trip to Croatia, and one of the country's signature seafood dishes that you absolutely cannot afford to miss is called Brudet, which is essentially the local take on a fish stew. A whole range of seafood can be used, and some local favourites include scorpion fish, mussels, conger eel and rockfish. This is combined with the fresh flavours of olive oil, tomato, garlic, and parsley.

32. Take in the Joy of Zadar's Quirky Sea Organ

To be honest, we are not exactly sure how to describe the Sea Organ in Zadar, because it's like nothing that we have ever seen before. We'd say that it's part architectural object and part art installation, but you really have to see it and experience it for yourself. It is a giant musical instrument set on the coast. As the waves lap against the shore, they enter into the tubes of the Sea Organ, and make a series of sounds – the city and ocean's own music.

33. Visit a 15th Century Castle in Northwest Croatia

When visiting Croatia, most people keep themselves to the main tourist spots such as Hvar, Dubrovnik, Split, and Zagreb, but get off the beaten track a little and you'll immerse yourself in a world virtually unexplored by tourists. Veliki Tabor Castle, nestled in the depths of the Croatian hills is one such example of an unexplored but beautiful site. This castle dates all the way back to the 15th century, and it's beautiful whether you visit in summer or winter. In the summer months, you'll experience a fairy tale vision with lush green hills, and in the wintertime a chillingly picturesque blanket of white snow.

(Košnički Hum 1, 49216, Desinić; www.veliki-tabor.hr)

34. Learn How to Make Pottery on Your Croatia Trip

Croatia is a wonderful place for ambling from place to place, but if you are a creative type who likes to be engaged with arty activities, why not pick up a new arts skill while you are in the country? The Raku Garden is a pottery studio on the charming island of Brac that offers exactly that opportunity. Their pottery courses are suitable for beginners, and while you're not spinning the potter's wheel you can take a dip in the ocean and explore the local fishing village.

(21413 Povlja, Brač; www.therakugarden.com)

35. Catch a Movie at Kino Europa

Although there is tonnes to see, do, and keep you entertained in Croatia, sightseeing can be an exhausting exercise, and there might be times when all you want to do is kick back with a great movie. When that moment comes, you need to know about Kino Europa in Zagreb, the oldest cinema in the city, with a commitment to showing independent arthouse movies that offer something different to the mainstream. It also hosts a number of film festivals, so be sure to keep up with their programme of events if you're a cinephile.

(Varšavska ul. 3, 10000, Zagreb; www.kinoeuropa.hr)

36. Dance, Dance, Dance at the InMusic Festival

Croatia is one of those places that attract visitors from all over Europe just so that they can attend the banging summer festivals. If you love nothing more than to dance with your hands in the air whilst breathing in fresh sea air, we can pretty much guarantee that you'll have a whale of a time at InMusic, Croatia's largest and most popular summer festival. All kinds of music are represented and previous acts that have taken to the stage include MGMT, Florence & The Machine, and Black Rebel Motorcycle Club.

(www.inmusicfestival.com/en)

37. Escape City Life at Zagreb's Maksimir Park

With a population of around 800,000 people, Zagreb isn't exactly an overwhelming city, but if you want to escape any cars or buildings for a morning, make sure that you immerse yourself in the expansive green of Maksimir Park.

This is Zagreb's oldest city park, covering a space of more than 1000 acres, and is landscaped in the style of an English garden with manicured lawns and winding pathways that are perfect for a stroll in the fresh air.

(Maksimirski perivoj, 10000, Zagreb; www.park-maksimir.hr)

38. Sample Croatian Craft Beers on Hvar Island

Although central and east European countries have a great reputation when it comes to beers, Croatian hasn't exactly made its mark on the beer map of Europe. But this is not to say that you can't find some yummy local ales, and one of the most charming local microbreweries is called Vunetovo, which you'll find on Hvar Island. It also has an outdoor terrace so you can sip on refreshing beers in the sunshine.

(Put Podstina 13, 21450, Hvar)

39. Take a Cable Car to the Peak of Mount Srd

When you are in Dubrovnik, you will undoubtedly notice a green mountain (or white if you're visiting in the winter) looming over the city. This is Mount Srd, and while it is possible to hike up the 400 metres or so of the mountain, a more relaxing way to make the trip is via a cable car that will take you all the way to the mountain peak in a matter of minutes. From the top, you can enjoy a view of the gorgeous white and orangey buildings of Dubrovnik, as well as the brilliantly blue sea beyond.

(www.dubrovnikcablecar.com)

40. Revive and Restore Yourself on Losinj Island

The stresses and responsibilities of everyday life can take their toll, and it's a great idea to use your vacation time to rest, recuperate, and really take care of your wellness. Well, there is truly no better place for this than Losinj island, which is known in Croatia for growing healing herbs, and for its astounding number of wellness retreats and spas. Whether you want some indulgent aromatherapy, healing massages, or revitalising facials, it's yours for the taking on Losinj.

41. Learn About Croatia's Greatest Sculptor at Mestrovic Gallery

Unless you are immersed in the Croatian art world, you probably won't be familiar with the name Ivan Mestrovic, but he is actually one of the most acclaimed artists and sculptors that's ever existed in Croatia. To get to grips with his works, passing a leisurely afternoon at the Mestrovic Gallery in Split is a wonderful idea. The collection includes sculptures, drawings, paintings, furniture, and architectural plans.

(Šetalište Ivana Meštrovića 46, 21000, Split; www.mestrovic.hr)

42. Be Stunned by a 4th Century Ancient Palace in Split

Whether you are somebody who loves to visit sites of historical importance or not, we think that it's impossible to not be carried away by all the incredible grandeur of the Diocletian's Palace in Split. This ancient palace was built by a Roman Emperor at the turn of the 4th century, half of which was used as his personal residence and half as a military garrison. The palace is the centre of Split, and is incredibly well preserved considering its history. It's also a filming location for Game of Thrones.

(www.diocletianspalace.org)

43. Take in a Show at the Croatian National Theatre

If you're the kind of person who loves to get all dressed up for a night at the theatre, be sure to keep up to date with the programme at the Croatian National Theatre in Zagreb, which is the best place in the whole of the country to catch a performance. The theatre dates all the way back to the 1860s and many incredible world-class performers have graced its stage, from the likes of Vivian Leigh to Laurence Olivier. It's particularly strong for opera and ballet.

(Trg maršala Tita 15, 10000, Zagreb; www.hnk.hr/en)

44. Get Close to Sea Life at Aquarium Pula

A country like Croatia with so much coastline is, of course, home to some incredible sea life. The best place to get up close to sea creatures and explore what's under the water without getting your feet week? Aquarium Pula. Enter this aquarium and you'll have the chance to get well acquainted with the waters of the Adriatic and all that lives in her. You'll find octopus, scorpion fish, lobsters, seahorses, and so much more besides. Kids will be entranced.

(Verudela bb, Verudela, 52105, Pula; www.aquarium.hr)

45. Learn About Olive Oil on Brac Island

Because Croatia is a Balkan country, it's often forgotten that it's also on the Mediterranean sea, and that it's very close to the warm climes of Italy. For this reason, Croatia is a producer of some of the most delicious olive oil, but it's a secret outside of Croatia. To get on board with the local olive oil culture, be sure to visit Brac Island, which is home to the Museum of Olive Oil. This is a private museum set in a family mill that dates way back to 1864. *(www.muzejuja.com)*

46. Peruse the Britanski Trg Antiques Market

Sundays can always be a little bit tricky when you are travelling. Museums tend to be closed, and cafes might not open until later in the day, but something fun that you can do with a free Sunday morning in Zagreb is head to the Britanski Trg Antiques Market. This is a place that few tourists know about, which means local prices and some truly incredible finds, whether you're after antique books or vintage jewellery. As with all antiques markets, it really pays to arrive early to seek out the best stuff.

47. Pay a Visit to the Oldest Working Pharmacy in Europe

Visiting a pharmacy while travelling probably doesn't seem like a good time at all. After all, nobody wants to feel sick while they're on their travels. But please do make an exception for the Old Pharmacy Museum in Dubrovnik, which is actually the oldest operational pharmacy in all of Europe, and it's been serving customers for an astounding 700 years. They also have some really cool displays of ancient lab equipment, historic medical books, and more intriguing curiosities.

(Placa 2, Dubrovnik)

48. Party on the Beach at Hula Hula Hvar

If you are a party person, we have no doubt that you are going to have a whale of a time during your stay in Croatia. Almost all of the main cities, but particularly the islands, cater to partygoers who travel from around Europe to enjoy the unique party lifestyle of Croatia. Our favourite spot to dance the night away on Hvar Island is Hula Hula Hvar. You'll find the bar sitting directly on the beach, so you can party the night away with sand between your toes, great music from the bar, and a cocktail in hand. *(Ul. Vlade Avelinija 10, Hvar; www.hulahulahvar.com)*

49. Enjoy the Clear Waters of Srebrna Bay

Whether you want to party hard or get away from it all, Croatia is a destination with something for every kind of traveller, and when we want an isolated spot away from the tourist crowds and with beautiful waters, we always head to Srebrna Bay on Vis Island. What we love most about this beach is the perfectly clear water that would make you think you're in the tropics rather than in Croatia. Pack a picnic and enjoy the solitude.

50. Climb to the Top of Anica Kuk

Are you the kind of person who lives for thrilling adventures that help you to appreciate the landscapes of a country in a whole new way? If so, there's no doubt that you need to know about Anica Kuk, the most formidable vertical rock within Paklenica National Park. It has a very high altitude of 712 metres, and since its almost completely vertical, it really offers a challenge to mountain climbers who have been returning to the rock for 70 years.

51. Dance Til Your Drop at Hideout Festival

There is no doubt that Croatia has made a huge impression of the festival summer circuit in the last decade or so, and if you love the idea of partying to incredible electronic music while soaking up the rays of the sun on a Croatian beach, Hideout Festival needs to be your next summer festival ticket. Lasting for 5 days and nights, and playing host to 150 artists, it's an epic party you won't ever forget. Talent that has played this festival includes Stormzy and Diplo, and it takes place on the island of Pag at the end of June each year.

(www.hideoutfestival.com)

52. Get Grisly at Zagreb's Museum of Torture

When you're on holiday, you know doubt want to forget about the troubles of the world, but we think that it's worth taking an afternoon out of drinking cocktails and ambling the cute streets to visit the Museum of Torture in Zagreb. The dark rooms of this museum contain instruments of torture as well as a number of replicas.

Seeing a guillotine, pendulum, or iron maiden up close is a sobering and fascinating experience.

(Radićeva ul. 14, 10000, Zagreb; http://tortureum.com)

53. Indulge a Science Geek at Tesla's Birthplace Museum

If you're something of a science geek, the name Nicola Tesla is no doubt already etched into your brain, belonging to the Croatian scientist best known for his contributions to the modern AC electrical supply system. Well, you can seriously geek out by heading to the birthplace museum of the man himself in Smiljan. It was in this small house where the great man first learned about electricity. Inside you'll learn about his provincial upbringing and his science obsessed life.

(www.mcnikolatesla.hr)

54. Take in the Views of the Istrian Peninsula from Vojak Peak

If you want to get off the beaten track while you're in Croatia, be sure to etch some time at the Istrian peninsula into your itinerary. It also has coastline, it has history, and has some great food, but people just don't seem to know about it. If you love either hiking or biking, be sure to make your way to Vojak Peak, which has some well marked paths, and some of the best views of the region. On a clear day, you can even look out onto Slovenia.

55. Rent a Scooter and Zoom Over Vis Island

Choosing between the islands of Croatia is no easy task, but we can't deny that the charm of Vis island has us thinking about its clear waters and tiny fishing villages right throughout the year. Because it's such an isolated place, making your way around the island can be a bit of a hassle. But not if you rent a scooter! This is a great idea – for feeling the wind in your face and exploring the hidden bays that you wouldn't otherwise be able to reach.

56. Cool Down With a Gelato From Luka Ice Cream in Split

Because it's part of the Balkans, people forget that the coastal areas of Split can get really quite hot in the summer months. Well, we don't know about you, but our favourite way to cool down in any location is with a heaped ice cream cone. And for an ice cream to remember, we recommend that you check out a place called Luka Ice Cream in Split. The flavour selection changes daily, and often contains treasures such as apple pie flavour, panacotta raspberry, and rosemary vanilla. Unbelievably good.

(Kroatien, Ul. Petra Svačića 2, 21000, Split; www.facebook.com/LukaIceCream)

57. Learn About Croatia's Oldest Settlement at Stari Grad Museum

Hvar Island is a place that attracts many tourists because of the beach parties and good food, but if you're a history buff, you can have more of a cultural experience on the island as well. The island's small town of Stari Grad is actually the oldest settlement in Croatia, and it's well worth taking a walk around and then visiting the Stari Grad Museum for an extra history lesson. The museum is a former 19th century palace, and still has interiors and furnishings from that period.

(Ul. Braće Biankini 4, 21460, Stari Grad; http://msg.hr)

58. Finish Your Meal With a Glass of Prosek

If you'd rather finish a meal with a refreshing drink than a sticky dessert, you need to know about Prosek, a drink that is only made in south Europe, and that's very popular in Croatia. This is a sweet dessert wine made with grapes that are dried to concentrate their juice and sweetness. A true glass of Prosek will always be at least 15% so it's also great if you want to relax into the evening and then have a great night of sleep!

59. Look to the Stars at Visnjan Observatory

If you are a bit of a science or astronomy geek, you will have full reign to geek out on a trip to Visnjan Observatory, which is located about 15 minutes away from Novigrad. Although it's pretty much in the middle of nowhere, this observatory is responsible for some of the most important astronomical discoveries that the world has ever known. In fact, around 1400 minor planets have been discovered from this site in the last decade alone.

(Ul. Istarska 5, 52463, Višnjan; http://astro.hr)

60. Have an Artsy Day at Zagreb's Museum of Contemporary Art

Although Croatia is not a huge name in the art world, this is not to say that there is no arts culture to be explored, and if you are crazy about the visual arts we think that you'll be very impressed with Zagreb's Museum of Contemporary Art. What we really love about this gallery is that there is a huge focus placed on young Croatian artists that the world really hasn't heard of. With more than 12,000 objects in the gallery, from installations to video to sculpture, there is tonnes to explore.

(Avenija Dubrovnik 17, 10000, Zagreb; www.msu.hr)

61. Take a Boat Trip From Pula to the Brijuni Islands

One of the loveliest things about visiting a country with as much coastline and islands as Croatia is the ability to take lots of lovely boat trips and really feel the ocean breeze on your face. We think that Pula to the unexplored Brijuni Islands makes for a very wonderful trip indeed, and the islands are a spectacular reward once you arrive. Only the largest of the islands can be visited, and it is a wild place, filled with rare plants such as wild cucumbers and marine poppies. Very special indeed.

62. Get Decadent With Black Truffles From Istria

When you're on holiday, it's time to get decadent and indulge in a way that would just never occur to you in your day-to-day life. And what is more decadent than the pungent, earthy, and savoury taste of truffles? Well, believe it or not, Croatia is a part of the world with quite a monopoly on all kinds of deliciousness, including truffles that come from the hardly visited Istria part of the country. It's possible to go on a truffle hunting adventure, but if you don't find any, this is still the place to sample all their incredible decadence.

63. Sip on Cocktails on a Cliff Face at Buza Bar

Let's face it, the grand sights and historic ruins of a country are all well and good, but what beats the sun shining down on you, looking out to a great view, and sipping on a cocktail? Fortunately, there is no shortage of views nor sunshine in Croatia. Buza Bar in Dubrovnik is one of the most special spots in Croatia for a sundowner, in our opinion. It's located on the edge of a cliff face, and offers a dramatic vista of the pounding ocean.

(Crijevićeva ul. 9, 20000, Dubrovnik)

64. Get Political at the Annual Subversive Festival

All of the nations that make up Former Yugoslavia are invariably very politically charged, and Croatia is certainly no exception. If you are somebody who is motivated by political movements and charged discussions, you'll feel right at home during Zagreb's annual Subversive Festival, a festival that's dedicated to political films and discussion. Each year takes on a different theme such as Decolonisation or The Politics of Friendship. It's hosted every May.

(http://subversivefestival.com/en)

65. Discover Ancient History at Grapceva Cave

Enter the Grapceva Cave, and you will be forgiven for thinking that you have entered into a completely different time in history. This cave, located on the island of Hvar, dates back to the New Stone Age, 4000-5000 years ago. The cave is filled with towering stalactites and stalagmites, with atmospheric hallways and chambers. This is one that you'll be impressed by whether you have an interest in ancient history or not.

66. Eat Lamb Fresh From the Spit at Sabunjar Restaurant

Something that you might notice while you're in Croatia is that lamb is probably the most popular meat amongst locals, and you'll no doubt be eating a hell of a lot of it while you're visiting. There are numerous ways to have lamb prepared, but we think it's at its tastiest when it is prepared on a rotating spit. This is quite a common way of preparing lamb in Croatia, and we particularly love the lamb at Sabunjar Restaurant in Zadar, a small city on the Dalmatian coast.

(Jadranska cesta, 23000, Zadar; http://restoran-sabunjar.hr/en/home-page)

67. Have a Sea Kayaking Adventure Off the Coast of Dubrovnik

When you think of Dubrovnik you no doubt think of the white and russet coloured buildings that contrast against the blue of the sky. But there is more to Dubrovnik than the city streets themselves, and you can also have plenty of adventures on the water. A great way to immerse yourself into the coastal seascape is by going on a sea kayaking adventure. With clear water beneath you, you'll have a stunning view of the city walls from the middle of the ocean.

68. Take in an Open Air Performance at the Dubrovnik Summer Festival

Dubrovnik is a gorgeous city at absolutely any time of year, but it is absolutely transformed with activity during the months of July and August thanks to all the fun of the Dubrovnik Summer Festival. This summer festival has been entertaining locals and tourists since 1950, and it offers a rich programme of classical music, dance performances, theatre, and opera in the open air of the city. There are many incredible site specific performances in places such as the steps of the Revelin Fortress and in front of the Rector's Palace.

(www.dubrovnik-festival.hr/en/node/34)

69. Get Artsy at Zagreb's Museum of Arts & Crafts

Stroll the aisles of Zagreb's Museum of Arts and Crafts and you will have a feast for the eyes. This museum dates all the way back to 1880, it started in a very small way but is now one of the most comprehensive arts museums in Zagreb, and completely dedicated to applied arts. The sheer number of kooky items on display is impressive. You'll find contemporary posters, vintage ball gowns, Baroque altar pieces, domestic ceramics, and so much more.

(Trg maršala Tita 10, 10000, Zagreb; www.muo.hr)

70. Take in the Glory of a 9th Century Church in Zadar

If church architecture is what it does for you, there is plenty to see around Croatia, and what we really love about the churches and cathedrals here is that many of them are out of the ordinary and really have a point of difference to other classical structures in Europe. The St Donatus Church in Zadar, for example, dates back to the 9th century, and stands out because of its unusual circular shape. It is one of few buildings from the Croatian Kingdom that survived the Mongol invasion of the 13th century.

71. Snorkel in the Waters Surrounding Vis Island

On a first visit to Croatia, something that you are bound to notice is just how clear the water is that surrounds many of the small islands. As well as being breathtakingly beautiful to look at, they are perfect for a snorkelling experience with lots of visibility. One of the islands best equipped for renting equipment and guiding you through the snorkelling experience is Vis. And when you make it to dry land, it's one of the best islands for seafood dishes!

72. Stop By a Winery With a View in Komarna

Wine lovers might first be tempted to visit France or Italy, and while these are, of course, wonderful countries for wine production, do not underestimate Croatia and its up-and-coming wine scene. If you are a true wine buff, you shouldn't miss the opportunity to visit a local winery, and we particularly love the Rizman Winery in Komarna. As well as beautiful wines, you'll be blown away by the hilltop views.

(Stolovi 2, 20356, Klek; www.rizman.com.hr/hr)

73. Visit a Stunning Dubrovnik Sight, Sponza Palace

If it's grand historic architecture that does it for you, there is no doubt that there is plenty to see in Dubrovnik, and one of the most sumptuous buildings would have to be Sponza Palace, which dates back to the 16th century. The palace has served a number of private and public functions during its history, but none so important as its function today because it now houses the Dubrovnik Archive, containing a huge wealth of materials pertaining to the city and its glorious history.

(Stradun 2, 20000, Dubrovnik;

www.tzdubrovnik.hr/lang/en/get/spomenici/5430/sponza_palace
.html)

74. Indulge a Sweet Tooth With a Slice of Kremsnita

When you're on holiday, it's time to get indulgent, and if you deny yourself sweet and creamy treats in your day-to-day life, be sure to treat yourself during your time in Croatia. And we can't think of a more delicious treat than a giant slice of Kremsnita, which is basically the Croatian take on a cream cake. This treat is most popular in Zagreb where you'll find it in all the bakeries and cafes. It consists of a puff pastry base, a custard cream centre, and chocolate icing on top. Yum!

75. Have the Party of Your Life Soundwave Festival

If you're somebody who loves to party hard and then party some more, Tisno is a town that you need to know about. Why? Because this is the festival capital of the country, playing host to about five different music festivals each and every summer. Soundwave is one of the most enduringly popular of these, mixing uplifting dance music, with art, performance and film. It takes place each year at the end of July, and is hosted in a serene and magical secluded bay.

(www.soundwavecroatia.com)

76. Put Your Foot to the Pedal on Losinj Island

With so many islands, Croatia somewhere to really explore and get to know some off the beaten track places. For an island where you won't be bumping into lots of tourists, try Losinj. This is well known as a place to get away from it all, and it's also a fantastic cycling destination with many cycle paths. There are cycle routes for all fitness levels, so whether you'd enjoy a gentle ride along the coast or you'd prefer something more challenging in the mountains, the choice is yours.

77. Catch a Croatian Film at Pula Film Festival

If you are a film buff through and through, be sure not to miss the Pula Film Festival, which is hosted in July each year. This film festival is special for a couple of reasons. First of all, it's the oldest film festival in Croatia, dating back to 1954, and secondly, it's hosted in Pula's Roman Amphitheatre, which has a history that dates all the way back to the 1st century. Most of the films are Croatian, so it's a good opportunity to get to know the local cinema culture.

(http://pulafilmfestival.hr)

78. Look at Gorgeous Glass Objects in Zadar

One of our favourite attractions in Zadar has to be a fairly new addition to the city's cultural scene: The Museum of Ancient Glass. It plays right into our love for looking at shiny, beautiful shimmering things, and the collection is simply stunning. Housed in a 19th century palace, the museum has a collection of Roman glassware to rival world-class museums, with vials, goblets, and jars retrieved from archaeological sites across Dalmatia. There are also replicas for sale in the museum shop, which make for unique gifts.

(www.mas-zadar.hr)

79. Hike Up Mosor Mountain for a Killer View

If you find yourself in Split, something that you are likely to notice on the horizon is the looming presence of Mosor Mountain. If you fancy escaping the city for a day and getting active, hiking to the peak of the mountain makes for an unforgettable day trip. As you hike up the mountain, you'll be greeted by donkeys and quaint stone houses that will take you back to a simpler time. And from the peak you'll have the most spectacular view of Split and beyond.

80. Get Decadent at a Michelin Star Restaurant, Monte in Rovinj

We can't pretend that Croatia is one of the cheapest travel spots in Europe, but we also think that it would be a shame to count your pennies at every turn and not to have at least a couple of indulgent experiences while you're in this magnificent country. And what could be a better way to splurge than paying for a decadent meal at a Michelin star restaurant? Monte in Rovinj is a spectacular restaurant, and with the tasting menu you can try lots of different bites and get some good value for money. *(Ul. Montalbano 75, 52210, Rovin; www.monte.hr)*

81. Have a Windsurfing Adventure at Bol

With so much coastline, Croatia is a place where you can have fun with all kinds of beach activities. So leave the sunbathing aside for an afternoon and try something different. In the coastal town of Bol, there is some of the very best windsurfing in Europe, perfect for anyone with an outdoorsy nature and adventurous spirit. Even if you have zero experience, there are plenty of schools that can show you the ropes so that you can enjoy this fun coastal activity.

82. Sip on Lots of Croatian Wine at Dubrovnik FestiWine

Croatia may not be the most famous place for wines in Europe, but there is still plenty to explore for wine lovers, and you can try lots of Croatian wines in one place if you make it to the Dubrovnik FestiWine festival. This is hosted each year in April, and it's considered the premiere wine event in the country. You'll get to taste a range of local wines, take part in tasting workshops with sommeliers, and buy a few bottles to take back home with you.

(www.dubrovnikfestiwine.com/en)

83. Immerse Yourself in the Beauty of Plitvice Lakes

One of the reasons that we love to visit Croatia is that even if you choose to do nothing, amble along the streets, and stare into space, you are surrounded by immense beauty at absolutely every turn. And a fine example of this is that the Plitvice Lakes, a 295 square kilometre forest reserve that is best known for its 16 terraced lakes. Walk the limestone canyon, have a sailing adventure on the lakes, bathe in one of the many waterfalls, and simply enjoy being in the presence of such natural beauty.

84. Warm Yourself From the Inside Out With a Plate of Pasticada

Every country has its special occasion dishes that are made for birthdays, holidays, and family gatherings. In the Dalmatian part of Croatia that dish would have to be pasticida, and this is essentially the Croatian version of a beef stew – only better than any other beef stew you have sampled before. The stew contains copious amounts of red wine, prunes, figs, and flavourings such as mustard, bay leaves, and rosemary. Perfect for a chilly evening.

85. Visit an Octagonal Roman Cathedral in Split

While in Split, you get the best of both beautiful coastline and incredible history and culture. One of the cultural sights that should not be missed is the Cathedral of St Domnius, which is actually the oldest Catholic Church that remains in use with its original structure. This beautiful church is unique in that it has an octagonal shape, and it dates all the way back to the 4th century. There are also many sacral artworks inside the church that date to the 13th century.

(Ul. Kraj Svetog Duje 5, 21000, Split)

86. Stroll the Two Streets of Hum, the World's Smallest Town

If you are the kind of person who likes to get off the beaten track and explore the unexplored, how about the world's smallest town? Yup, Croatia is home to a teeny tiny place called Hum, and this town has a total of two streets. Of course, it can be explored very quickly, but that doesn't make it any less charming. Located in the Istria region, it has a total of 26 inhabitants, and it's a great place to pick up some local homemade brandy.

87. Stay Aboard a Botel in the Marina of Rijeka

As you travel around Croatia, you are likely to stay in a mixture of hotels, guesthouses, and hostels. There's absolutely nothing wrong with those choices, but if you fancy having more of a unique overnight experience, we'd love to recommend Botel, which you will find in the Marina of Rijeka. This old ferry boat is completely renovated, docked in the marina, and we think there's no better place to top up a tan than on the terrace with a view of the boats and Rijeka town.

(Riva, 51000, Rijeka; www.botel-marina.com)

88. Help Yourself to Platefuls of Yummy Octopus Salad

In the heat of a Croatian summer, you'll want to eat plates of light and refreshing food that don't weight you down. But salads are just boring, right? Err, not in Croatia! Forget limp lettuce and soggy cucumber, Croatia knows how to do a salad, and you'll figure this out as soon as you tuck into octopus salad, something that locals are known to enjoy on the coast. It's a simple dish comprising grilled octopus, boiled potatoes, olive oil, garlic, and capers.

89. Enjoy the Relaxed Festivities of Obonjan Festival

Croatia is a country that is well known for its epic summer festivals, but what if you'd like to enjoy a more laid back festival vibe that isn't quite so hardcore? Well, then you make your way to little known Obonjan Island where there is a festival that lasts the entire summer. Yes, there will be some relaxed parties on the beach, but you can also enjoy lots more holistic activities. Think sunset yoga on the beach, massage courses, and introductions to aromatherapy.

90. Enjoy Typical Comfort Food From Zagreb, Strukli

Although Croatia isn't such a large country, there are quite a few different types of terrain and different cultures, and this means that you can find different food in different places. A dish that is native to the Croatian capital of Zagreb is Strukli, which is basically a baked pastry filled with a creamy filling. The filling usually consists of cottage cheese, eggs, and sour cream, and it's the perfect thing to warm you up and give your stomach joy on a chilly Zagreb evening.

91. Be Stunned by the Waterfalls of Krka National Park

Looking to be stunned by all kinds of natural beauty in the wild of Croatia? Then look no further than Krka National Park, which has a ridiculous number of beautiful waterfalls, and let's be real, who doesn't love a waterfall? There are many falls to explore within the park, but the most famous of them all is the Skradinski Buk falls, a collection of waterfalls that have the most perfect blue-green water, they have a height of 45 metres, and offer plenty of space for a relaxing swim.

(www.npkrka.hr)

92. Keep the Kids Happy at Aquapark Istralandia

Croatia is a country that has it all, no matter what you want your holiday to be. Even kids will have a great time! If they don't enjoy walking around historic attractions, you can keep them entertained at a waterpark called Aquapark Istralandia. This park has the largest wave pool in all of the Mediterranean, 24 attractions with 1.6 kilometres of tunnels and shoots, as well as summertime concerts and shows.

(Ul. Ronko 1, 52474, Nova Vas; www.istralandia.hr)

93. Party on Pag Island at Sonus Festival

Crazy about techno music? Love nothing more than to party hard in a beautiful setting? Then the Sonus Festival will be right up your alley. Located on Pag Island, which is quiet and unspoiled, it transforms during the festival to become a techno lover's dream come true. The festival has only been going for five years or so, but it's already a major draw for Europe's party goers. It takes place at the end of August, and music talent at Sonus has included Jamie Jones and the Martinez Brothers.

(www.sonus-festival.com)

94. Tuck Into a Festive Snack of Fritules

Most people tend to visit Croatia during the summer months when they can soak up the sun, but we think that the time leading up to Christmas has a charm all of its own, and not least because of the delicious Christmas food. Fritules is something enduringly popular to eat in the festive period. It can be compared to a doughnut, but in reality it's so much more. The batter is flavoured with rum and citrus, and you can find raisins inside and lashings of powdered sugar on top.

95. Ride the Rapids of the Cetina River

When thinking about Croatia, it's easy to imagine all of your time exploring the city walls and the beautiful beaches, but look a little bit more inland, and you can find some spectacular nature. The Cetina River is 100 kilometres long and cuts right through the country. A walk along the river is never a bad thing, but something more exciting is a rafting adventure on the white water rapids of the Cetina. There are grade two and three rapids, so be prepared for a bumpy ride.

96. Say Hi to the Animals at Zagreb Zoo

Zagreb is a city with lots of museums and a tonne of culture to explore, but when you want to escape the bricks and mortar of the city for a day, Zagreb Zoo, the biggest zoo in Croatia, is a great way to get back to nature and close to some animals. The zoo is home to more than 2000 animals across over 200 species, and some of the animals you might see include the North China leopard, the red panda, and the Bactrian camel.

(Maksimirski perivoj, 10000, Zagreb; http://zoo.hr)

97. Experience a Local Croatian Carnival in Samobor

When you think of carnival celebrations you would no doubt first think of the streets of Rio and its colourful parades, but believe it or not there are also some carnival festivities to be found in Croatia. Samobor is a suburb of Zagreb city, and it's not usually a place of huge excitement, but all that changes during the Easter week. You'll find a wonderful street parade, full of people dressed up wearing masks, and the burning of Fasnik, which represents the letting go of any bad things that happened in the last year.

98. Feel Zagreb's Creative Pulse at Lauba

Although Zagreb is the capital of Croatia, it often gets neglected in favour of places like Dubrovnik and Split. While those are certainly beautiful cities, if you want to feel the creative heartbeat of Croatia, the capital city is the place to be. And there is nowhere that you'll feel that creative energy more strongly than at Lauba, a contemporary art gallery located in a former textile mill. Inside, you'll see works by contemporary Croatian artists from the 1950s onwards.

(Filipovića 23, 10000, Zagreb; www.lauba.hr/en)

99. Allow Your Cares to Slide Away at the Samovar Tea Shop

There is so much to see and do in Croatia, but sometimes to just need to take a breather and relax with a hot cup of tea. When that moment comes, you should head straight for the Samovar Tea Shop in the small coastal city of Rijeka. This charming little spot is filled with teas from all over the world, and the staff are incredibly passionate about what they sell.

(Užarska ul. 14, 51000, Rijeka; www.samovar.hr)

100. Find Vintage Treasures at Hrelic, Zagreb

While in Croatia, you'll no doubt want to have a few shopping experiences so that you can buy a few items to remind you of your visit. Take our advice and avoid the sanitised malls and tacky tourist shops and head to Zagreb's Hrelic flea market instead. Sellers rock up with their vans, and sell all kinds of cool and kooky items, from vintage posters to handmade jewellery. We particularly love the market in the winter, when the whole place is blanketed with snow.

(Sajmišna cesta, 10010, Zagreb)

101. Learn How to Cook Croatian Dishes at Le Mandrac

We're certain that you will be bowled over by the incredible local cuisine while you're in Croatia. Whether you love barbecues, fresh seafood, or pastries, there is something for every palette, but how much cooler would it be if you actually knew how to make delicious Croatian food from scratch? Well, Le Mandrac restaurant in the coastal town of Opatija offers lessons so that you can impress your friends with a Croatian themed dinner party when you get home.

(Obala F. Supila 10, 51410, Volosko/Opatija)

Before You Go…

Thanks for reading **101 Amazing Things to Do in Croatia.** We hope that it makes your trip a memorable one!

Have a great trip!

Team 101 Amazing Things

Made in the USA
Monee, IL
10 December 2022